STORYTELLER: HINDU STORIES

Anita Ganeri

Illustrations by Carole Gray

TULIP
BOOKS®

www.tulipbooks.co.uk

Introduction

Hindu Stories

In each of the world's six main religions - Hinduism, Judaism, Buddhism, Christianity, Islam and Sikhism - stories play a very important part. They have been used for many hundreds of years to teach people about their faith in a way which makes difficult messages easier to understand. Many stories tell of times in the lives of religious teachers, leaders, gods and goddesses. Others explain mysterious events such as how the world was created or what happens when we die. Many have a strong moral or lesson to teach.

The collection of stories in this book comes from the Hindu scriptures. Hinduism began in India at least 5000 years ago. Hindus believe that everything comes from a spirit called Brahman. It is the source of all life and is eternal. Hindus often call Brahman God. They also believe that there are many gods and goddesses and that each one is a different way of showing Brahman. In this book, you can read some of the stories about the Hindu gods and goddesses.

Contents

How the World Came to Be

Long, long ago, Lord Vishnu created the different universes and in each universe, he lay down on an ocean of milk. A pure, white lotus flower came from his navel and, fast asleep, inside its satin petals, lay Lord Brahma, the creator, the source of all things. While Lord Brahma slept, there was nothing. Then Brahma stirred and woke up, and began to create the world and everything in its four quarters.

First, he created the gods of the sky. They were Soma, the moon and Surya, the sun. He placed them in the heavens to bring night and day. Then he created Agni, god of fire, Vayu, the wind and Varuna, the ocean.

Into the ocean, Lord Brahma placed a gleaming, golden egg. Gently rocking on the waves, the egg grew and grew. For a whole year it grew...until, one day, it started to crack, wider and wider, until it split right open. From its golden inside Lord Brahma stepped out, crowned in shining light. He divided the egg into two halves and placed one above as the arch of the sky, and one below as the earth. Then he made human beings to live on the earth, in the golden shell of the empty egg.

And so the world was made. But when Lord Brahma falls asleep again, his creation will dissolve into nothing and the world we know will no longer exist.

Did you know?

Hindus usually worship God at home as well as in the mandir (temple). They offer flowers, food and incense to images or pictures of the gods and goddesses. They believe that the gods and goddesses are different forms and aspects of God. They receive God's blessing in return.

Did you know?

There are thousands of Hindu gods and goddesses. Three of the most important are Brahma, Vishnu and Shiva. Brahma (see picture) is the creator of the world. Vishnu is the protecter. Shiva is in charge of destroying the uni- verse ready for it to be created again.

The God and the Wicked Witch

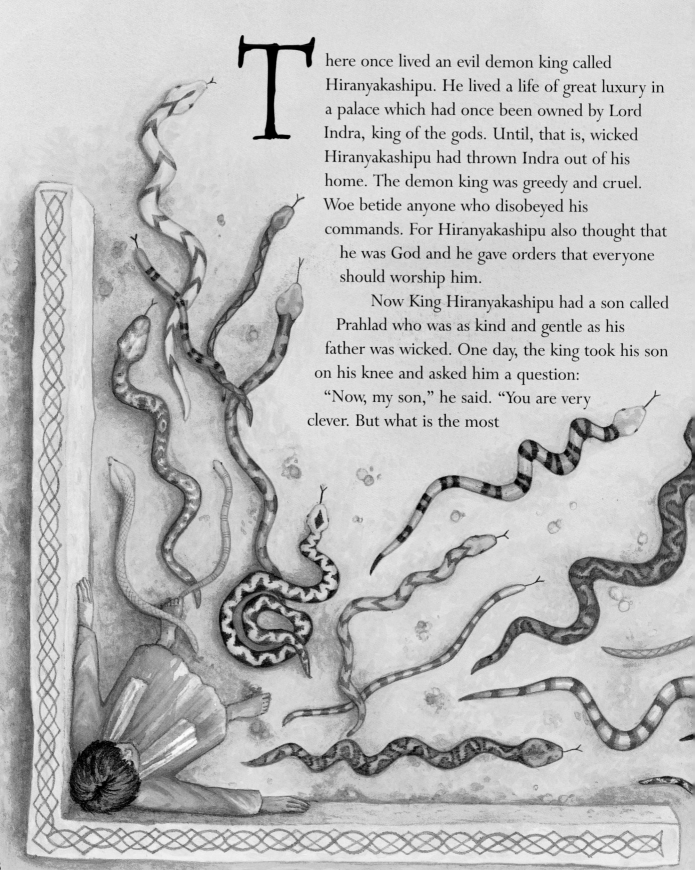

There once lived an evil demon king called Hiranyakashipu. He lived a life of great luxury in a palace which had once been owned by Lord Indra, king of the gods. Until, that is, wicked Hiranyakashipu had thrown Indra out of his home. The demon king was greedy and cruel. Woe betide anyone who disobeyed his commands. For Hiranyakashipu also thought that he was God and he gave orders that everyone should worship him.

Now King Hiranyakashipu had a son called Prahlad who was as kind and gentle as his father was wicked. One day, the king took his son on his knee and asked him a question:

"Now, my son," he said. "You are very clever. But what is the most important thing you have learned at school?"

"That you are the king," replied Prahlad. "But Lord Vishnu is God, and he is greater than everyone."

His father was furious.

"How dare you!" he bellowed, throwing Prahlad off his knee. "Lord Vishnu, pah! You must worship me!" he shouted.

"No, father," Prahlad said, very calmly. "I must worship Lord Vishnu."

King Hiranyakashipu decided that Prahlad must be punished. He ordered his soldiers to take him away and throw him from the top of a cliff. But Lord Vishnu was watching over Prahlad and the boy floated gently to the ground, like a feather.

"Throw him in front of an elephant!" the king shrieked. So the soldiers threw Prahlad in the path of a charging elephant. But, again, Lord Vishnu protected Prahlad and the elephant stopped and bowed down in front of him.

Next, the soldiers threw Prahlad into a pit full of poisonous snakes but the snakes would not bite him. Then they charged at him with their swords but even the sharp, steel blades could not pierce him. They simply could not hurt the boy. Lord Vishnu was always protecting Prahlad, who smiled as he remembered his Lord.

The soldiers finally admitted defeat and dragged the boy back to his father.

"Now will you worship me?" shouted the king.

"No, dear father, " said Prahlad, "I worship Lord Vishnu. He has been looking after me."

The king was livid. How dare Prahlad defy him? In a terrible temper, he went to see his sister, a wicked witch called Holika.

"That boy needs teaching a lesson," she cackled, "and I've got just the thing."

And this is what the evil pair did. They built a huge bonfire in the palace grounds and lit it to make a roaring blaze. Then Holika called to Prahlad.

"Dear nephew," she sneered. "Let's play a game. Come and walk into this fire with me. Come on, now, you won't get burned. My magic powers will protect us."

For Holika had a boon (promise) from Agni, the fire god, that she could not be hurt by fire. But of course, she planned to leave Prahlad in the fire to burn while she walked out unharmed. The two walked into the bonfire. But, as so many times before, ▶

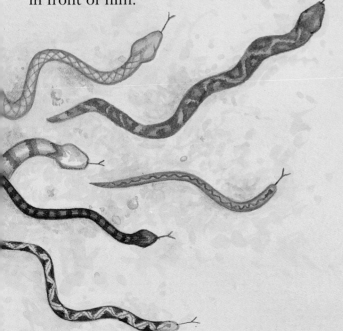

Lord Vishnu was watching over Prahlad. Quick as a flash, he snatched Prahlad out of the flames and left his wicked aunt Holika to perish.

And to this day, whenever there is danger from enemies, people remember how Lord Vishnu rescued Prahlad and pray for Lord Vishnu's protection.

STORYTELLERSTORYTELLERSTORYTELLERST

Did you know?

In February or March, Hindus celebrate the festival of Holi. It marks the end of winter and welcomes in spring. It is also a time for remembering the story of Prahlad. On the night before Holi, a big bonfire is lit to remind people of the fate of Holika, the wicked witch, who gave the festival its name.

Rama Rescues Sita

Long ago, King Dasharatha ruled the kingdom of Kosala in India from his capital in the city of Ayodhya. He was a good and just king, and ruled his kingdom wisely and well. Prince Rama was the eldest of his four sons. He was handsome, brave and dutiful, the apple of his father's eye. Rama married a beautiful princess called Sita. Filled with pride and delight in his favourite son, Dasharatha made him heir to the throne. But Rama's stepmother had other plans. She went to see King Dasharatha.

"Long ago, my Lord, I saved your life in battle," she said, "and in return, you gave me two boons to ask from you whenever I liked. Now it is time to keep your promises. The first is to make my son, Bharata, king, instead of Rama. The second is to banish Rama to the forest for fourteen years."

The heartbroken king had no choice but to keep his word, and sadly Rama obeyed his father's wishes. He left his home and set off for the forest with Sita and his brother, Lakshman.

Many years passed. Rama, Sita and Lakshman lived happily in a cottage in the forest and collected wild fruit and vegetables to eat. One day, Rama and Lakshman were out trying to catch a golden deer which Sita had spotted among the trees. It was the most beautiful creature she had ever seen and she wanted to keep it as a pet. While they were gone, an old man came to the door. He was dressed as a wandering holy man.

"Is anyone there?" he called, "to welcome a poor stranger?"

Sita opened the door and welcomed the holy man in. This was the chance he had been waiting for. For this was no ordinary stranger. It was the terrifying ten-headed Ravana, demon king of Lanka, in disguise. It was he who had sent the golden deer to trick Rama and Lakshman, and keep them out of his wicked way. He grabbed Sita by the hand and bundled her into his chariot. Then he sped through the skies back to Lanka, for he had been told that if he married Sita, he would rule the world.

When Rama and Lakshman returned, they were filled with grief and dismay. ▶

11

For days and days, they searched the forest, but Sita was nowhere to be found. In despair, Rama called on the monkey army to help him find his wife. The monkeys searched high and low for Sita but they could not find her anywhere, until they came to the southernmost tip of India and met Sampathi, the vulture.

"I can tell you where Sita is," the vulture croaked. "Ravana has carried her off to Lanka."

Now Lanka was an island, far out in the ocean. To reach Sita, they would first have to cross the sea. From their ranks, the monkeys chose the general, Hanuman, for this dangerous task. Now Hanuman was no ordinary monkey. He was the son of the god of the wind. He took a huge, running jump and, with a single bound, leapt over the water to Lanka. On and on he flew until he reached Ravana's magnificent palace, decorated with jewels stolen from the gods. Then, as quietly as a mouse, he crept inside and found Sita kept prisoner in the palace garden, watched over by demon guards. Sita was overjoyed to see him. She gave him her ring to take back to Rama.

"Please come and rescue me soon," she whispered to Hanuman. "For if I don't agree to marry Ravana, he has vowed to eat me for supper."

"Don't worry, my lady," promised Hanuman, "we will soon come back for you." ▶

STORYTELLERSTORYTELLERSTORYTELLERSTORYTELLERSTORYTELLERSTORYTELLERSTORYTELLE

Did you know?

The story of Rama and Sita comes from a long poem called the Ramayana. It has 24,000 verses and is one of the Hindus' most sacred texts. The Ramayana is thought to have been first composed some 5000 years ago, although it was not written down until much later. It is still very popular today. In India, children can read the story in comic books and watch it on television.

Then, bidding her farewell, he sped back over the sea back to Rama and told him all that he had seen and heard.

When Rama and Lakshman heard Hanuman's news, they gathered a huge army of monkeys and bears, led by Hanuman and Jambhavan, king of the bears. Then they built a great bridge over the sea and marched all the way to Lanka. Meanwhile, in Lanka, Ravana was waiting. For his spies had told him that Rama was coming. He summoned all his best generals, demon soldiers and fierce giants, and sent them into battle.

"And don't come back until you've killed them all!" Ravana screamed after them.

All day and night, the battle raged. Soon the air was thick with the soldiers' cries, and with arrows and spears flung from both sides. By morning, the ground was red with blood and littered with the bodies of soldiers. Hanuman wept as he looked over the battlefield and saw so many friends lying injured or dead, but worse was to come. Suddenly, he spotted the bodies of Rama and Lakshman lying among the wounded. Hanuman knew that he had to act quickly. Fast as the wind, he flew away to a mountain in the Himalayas to pick some magic healing herbs. But he could not find the right herbs to pick so he lifted up the whole mountain instead and flew back to the battlefield with it. Soon not only were Rama and his brother brought back to health but all the other soldiers who had fallen in battle.

Did you know?

In October or November, Hindus celebrate the festival of Diwali. This is a very happy time when people remember the story of Rama and Sita, and light little oil lamps to welcome the couple home. Diwali celebrations last for five days. During this time, people visit the mandir, eat special food and exchange gifts and cards. There are also firework displays.

Now, at last, it was time for Rama to face Ravana alone. Ravana put on his finest gold armour, and strapped a golden helmet on each of his ten heads. Then he boarded his chariot and, with a blood-curdling battle cry raced off towards Rama. But Rama was ready for him. Calmly, he fitted a golden arrow into his bow, took careful aim and fired. The arrow, a gift sent by the gods, struck Ravana straight in the heart. With a frightful shriek, he toppled out of his chariot, dead.

Among the cheers and rejoicing, Sita came out of the palace to be reunited with Rama, her beloved husband. Then, together with Lakshman and faithful Hanuman, they rode back home to Ayodhya on a great swan, to be crowned king and queen.

Did you know?

Rama is a very popular Hindu god, worshipped for his bravery and goodness. He is actually Lord Vishnu in a different form. Hindus believe that Vishnu visits the Earth from time to time to save it from danger. Each time he takes a different form. These are Matsya, the fish; Kurma, the tortoise; Varaha, the boar; Narasingh, the man-lion; Vamana, the dwarf; Parashurama, the warrior; Lord Rama, the ideal king; Lord Krishna, the cowherd boy (see page 19); Lord Buddha, the teacher; and Kalki, the rider on a white horse who is still to appear on earth.

The Birth of the Blue God

On the banks of the Yamuna River in India, lay the kingdom of Mathura, which was ruled over by wicked King Kamsa. The king was unjust and unpopular but nobody dared disobey his orders. They were much too afraid of what he would do. The only good thing about King Kamsa was his beautiful sister, Devaki, who was kind and sweet to everyone. She lived at court with her husband, Vasudeva.

One day, when the three of them were together, King Kamsa heard a voice calling to him. It seemed to be coming from the sky.

"Beware, oh king," it whispered. "Beware of your sister's children. For the eighth child will one day kill you."

Then the voice was gone. King Kamsa was startled and a little bit frightened. What if the voice was telling the truth? He decided that the best thing to do was to kill his sister to make sure the prophecy could not happen. There and then, he drew out his sword. But Vasudeva begged the wicked king to change his mind.

"Spare her life, I beg you," Vasudeva pleaded, "and take our children instead. We will give them to you when they are born."

King Kamsa agreed. To make sure that Devaki and Vasudeva, and their children, could not escape, he threw them into prison and had them guarded day and night.

And so matters went on for several years. Devaki had seven babies and wicked Kamsa killed them, one by one. From his home in heaven, Lord Vishnu saw what was

happening and knew what must be done.

"I shall have myself born as Devaki's eighth child," said Vishnu. "I will be born as the baby Krishna." ▶

Did you know?

Each year, Hindus celebrate Krishna's birthday with a joyful festival called Janamashtami. It is held in August or September. A small cradle is placed in the mandir and covered with a cloth. At midnight, the time when Krishna is said to have been born, the cloth is taken away to show an image of baby Krishna inside.

How the Holy River Fell From Heaven

There was once a wise and just king called Sagara who had 60,000 sons. All of them were brave and strong, and devoted to their father.

Now the time came for King Sagara to perform the great horse sacrifice to show that he was the greatest king on earth. He chose the most splendid horse in his kingdom and set it free to wander as it pleased for one year. If it roamed into another kingdom, that king had to wage war against Sagara or accept him as the new ruler. King Sagara was certain of victory. At the end of the year, the horse would be sacrificed.

But just as the horse galloped off, a dreadful thing happened. Indra, the king of the gods, was worried that King Sagara was growing too powerful and might want to take his place. So he stole the horse and hid it deep underground, tethered behind a sage (wise man) called Kapila. The wise man had chosen this quiet place, far away from the earth, for his meditations. King Sagara's sons tried to comfort their father.

"Don't worry, Father," they said. "We'll find your horse and bring it back. No matter how long it takes."

So they set off. They dug a deep hole in the ground and found the horse and the sage. But the sage was so angry at being disturbed that, with one fiery glance, he reduced almost all of King Sagara's 60,000 sons to ashes. Only one of the sons survived. He returned home, with the horse, and helped his father to finish the sacrifice. Some time later, King Sagara gave up his throne and made his grandson, Bhagiratha, king in his place.

When Bhagiratha heard the story of his ancestors, he was filled with dismay. He made it his mission to help their souls gain salvation, so that they could finally go to heaven. But how was he to do it? He went to the temple to pray to Lord Vishnu.

"Lord Vishnu," he said. "I beg you to help me. The only way to save my ancestors is for the river of heaven to fall to Earth and wash their souls clean and pure."

Lord Vishnu took pity on the unhappy king. He ordered Ganga, the river goddess, to fall down from heaven. But Ganga did not want to be moved and Vishnu grew impatient. He gave the goddess a good nudge with his toe to send her on her way. This made Ganga very angry, and she began roaring and crashing to Earth in a rage.

Lord Shiva knew that if Ganga hit the ground in such a fury, the earth would shatter under her weight. So he caught the river in his long, thick hair and tangled Ganga up in knots so that she could not escape. When the goddess had calmed down, Shiva slowly untied his hair and let her trickle gently down to earth. Then King Bhagiratha led the river right across India and deep down under the ground. There its sacred water touched his ancestors' ashes and freed their souls from the endless cycle of birth and death so that they could find peace.

STORYTELLERSTORYTELLERSTORYTELLERSTORYTELLERSTORYTELLERSTORYTELLERSTORYTELLE

Did you know?

The river of heaven is called the Ganges. It flows from the Himalayas right across India until it reaches the sea at the Bay of Bengal. For Hindus, the Ganges is a holy river. They believe that even a drop of its water can wash away their sins. The sacred city of Varanasi is built on the banks of the river. Here the water is thought to be especially holy and powerful. Millions of people flock here to bathe. Legend says that Lord Shiva chose Varanasi to be his favourite home on Earth.

Ganesh, the Elephant God

The great god, Shiva, and his beautiful wife, the goddess Parvati, lived on a snow-capped mountain in the mighty Himalayas. They loved each other very much and were usually very happy. But Shiva often went away for years on end to meditate in the mountains and poor Parvati got very lonely and bored, waiting for him to return.

One day, Parvati was sitting in her palace, feeling sorry for herself. What was the point of being a goddess, she thought, if all you did was sit by yourself every day? Suddenly, she had a brilliant idea.

"I know," she said, with a happy smile. "I'll make myself a baby. He will keep me company."

So she collected some earth and some water and mixed them to make soft clay. Then she shaped the clay into a baby boy. She gave him a head, arms and legs, and a body with a round tummy. She marked his eyes, nose and mouth. Then she sprinkled the baby with holy Ganges water and brought him to life. Slowly, the baby opened one big, brown eye, then the other, then he began to smile. Parvati was overjoyed, and from that day on, she never went anywhere without her son whom she called Ganesh.

Several more years went by and still Shiva had not come home but Parvati now had her son to play with. She didn't have time to be lonely anymore. Then, one day, Parvati and her son went for a walk. It was a very hot day and Parvati stopped to take a dip in a cool mountain pool.

"Can you keep guard?" she asked her son. "Don't let anyone near now, will you?"

The boy sat down on a nearby rock.

A few minutes later, a tall figure walked by. It was none other than Shiva, hurrying home to see Parvati. He heard the sound of singing coming from the pool and recognised Parvati's voice. But he found his path blocked by a strange, little boy.

"Let me go past," he ordered the boy.

"I will not," the boy replied.

Shiva began to lose his temper. He was used to getting his own way. ▶

Did you know?

In August or September, Hindus celebrate Ganesh's birthday. They call this festival Ganesh Chaturthi. To mark this happy day, they visit the mandir or worship Ganesh at home. They offer him gifts of sweets and coconuts. On the last day of the festival, they carry clay images of Ganesh down to the river or sea. They say prayers, then dunk the images into the water.

23

"I'm going to give you one last chance," he raged. "Now let me go past."

"I will not," replied the boy.

Shiva was furious. Quick as a flash, he drew out his sword and, with a 'swish', cut the boy's head clean off.

When Parvati saw what had happened she screamed and then began to cry.

"You wicked man," she sobbed. "You've killed our son."

"What son?" said Shiva, in dismay. "We haven't got a son!"

"No, not any more!" sobbed Parvati. Then she explained what she'd done. "I got so lonely," she said, "that I made a baby. And now you've gone and killed him!"

Shiva was horrified. How could he make things better? After all, he loved Parvati very much and hated seeing her so unhappy. He promised to do anything Parvati wanted. Absolutely anything.

"You can bring our son back to life," she said, "or I'll never speak to you again."

So Shiva set off down the mountain and went into the forest to find a new head for his son. The first creature he saw was a magnificent elephant. He cut off its head and took it home, and fitted it on to the little boy's body. Then he breathed on him gently to wake him up. And that is how Ganesh got his elephant's head. Parvati was delighted.

"Now you'll be as wise and strong as an elephant," she said, with a smile.

Did you know?

Ganesh is one of the best-loved Hindu gods. He is worshipped as the god of wisdom and is thought to be able to take away obstacles and solve difficult problems. Whenever people start something new, like getting married, moving house or going on a journey, they ask Ganesh to bless them. In some parts of India, people paint pictures of Ganesh on their walls or above their doors to bring good luck.

Durga and the Buffalo Demon

Once, long ago, there lived a terrible demon whose name was Mahish. He was the strongest and bravest of all of the demons who lived on earth, causing misery and mischief wherever he went. Now Mahish had been granted a special favour by Lord Brahma - that he could only be killed by a woman. Otherwise he would live for ever. One day, the demon chiefs went to ask Mahish for his help.

"O great Mahish," they pleaded. "Once we were lords of all heaven but the gods came and stole our kingdom. No one can match you for strength and power. Please help us win it back."

Mahish agreed to help them, and set off with his army to the city of the gods. For one hundred years, the gods and demons fought a bloodthirsty battle which the demons finally won. Then the gleeful demons threw the gods out of heaven and made Mahish their king. In great dismay, the gods met together.

"We must get rid of this monster," they all agreed. "Once and for all." But how would they be able to do this? All the gods shut their eyes, and summoned all their powers together to call for help. Slowly, out of the gloom, a brilliant light appeared and a figure rode out of it, mounted on a roaring lion and shining like the sun. Her name was Durga, the warrior goddess. ▶

Did you know?

Durga is another name for Parvati, the wife of Shiva. She is a fierce and powerful goddess. In statues and pictures, like the one below, she is shown with many arms. These are for holding the weapons given to her by the gods to fight against the demons. Among the weapons are a bow and arrow, a discus (a spinning disc with a very sharp edge), a trident (three-pronged spear), and a sharp, curved sword. Durga rides on a lion or tiger, and blows a conch shell to summon her warriors into battle.

The gods gave Durga their deadliest weapons. Then she rode off towards Mahish's palace to challenge the demons to battle.

"I'll show those gods," Mahish sneered. "I'm not afraid of them."

From all sides, the demons charged towards her, attacking her army with spears and swords. But Durga's lion killed them, one by one, and gobbled them all down, until the demon army was completely destroyed and only Mahish was left. But clever Mahish was not beaten yet. Quick as a flash, he turned himself into a gigantic buffalo and charged into the middle of Durga's army. The earth shook under his pounding hooves. He uprooted the mountains with his horns, and tossed them high into the air. He whipped the sea into towering waves, with his lashing tail. It was a terrifying sight to see.

Durga took out a rope and caught the buffalo in a lassoo. But the buffalo turned into a lion and slipped out of the noose. Then, as Durga tried to catch him again, he changed from a lion to a man, from a man to an elephant, then back into a buffalo. Now Durga seized her chance. She pinned the buffalo down with her foot, and just as he turned back into a demon, she sliced off his head with her sword. Lord Brahma's promise had come true. Mahish had been killed by a woman.

So the gods returned to their rightful place in heaven, and danced and sang to celebrate Durga's great victory which had brought peace and harmony back to the world.

STORYTELLER
Did you know?

Each year, at the festival of Durga Puja, Hindus remember Durga's great victory over the demon. They visit the mandir to offer food and flowers to a special image of the goddess. At the end of the festival, the image is taken through the town and dunked into a river or pond. Durga Puja falls in September or October.

28

Glossary

Agni The Hindu god of fire who carries messages between the gods and people on Earth.

Brahma One of the three most important Hindu gods. He is the creator of the world.

Brahman The supreme soul or spirit. Brahman is eternal and present in everything. Hindus often call Brahman God.

Diwali The festival when Hindus remember the story of Rama and Sita. It is celebrated in October or November.

Durga The warrior goddess who kills the buffalo-demon Mahish and helps save the world.

Durga Puja The festival when Hindus remember Durga's victory over the demon Mahish.

Ganesh The elephant-headed god. He is the god of travellers and good fortune. Hindus worship him when they start something new.

Ganesh Chaturthi The festival when Hindus remember Ganesh's birthday. It is celebrated in August or September.

Ganges The holy river of the Hindus. It flows across India, from the Himalayas to the Bay of Bengal.

Hanuman The monkey god. He is Rama's loyal general and faithful friend. He is believed to be very brave and strong.

Himalayas A huge range of mountains that stretches across the north of India and Nepal. They are thought to be the homes of the gods.

Hinduism The religion of the Hindus.

Hindus Followers of the Hindu religion. Most Hindus live in India where Hinduism began at least 5000 years ago.

Holi A festival when Hindus remember the story of Holika, the wicked witch. It also marks the coming of spring and remembers times from Krishna's childhood. It is celebrated in February or March.

Indra The king of the gods.

Janamashtami A festival when Hindus remember Krishna's birthday. It is celebrated in August or September.

Krishna One of the most popular Hindu gods. He is a form of Lord Vishnu.

Lanka The home of Ravana on what we now call Sri Lanka, an island off the southern tip of India.

Mahish A terrible demon who caused chaos in the world. He turned into a buffalo and was killed by Durga.

Mandir A place where Hindus worship. It is also called a temple.

Parvati A powerful goddess and Shiva's wife.

Radha Krishna's wife

Rama One of the most popular Hindu gods. He is a form of Lord Vishnu.

Ramayana A long poem which is part of the Hindu scriptures. It tells the story of Rama and Sita.

Ravana The demon king who kidnaps Sita and takes her to Lanka.

Shiva One of the three most important Hindu gods. He is the destroyer of evil in the world.

Sita Rama's wife

Varanasi A city in northern India which is especially holy for Hindus. It lies on the banks of the River Ganges.

Vishnu One of the three most important Hindu gods. He is the protector of the world.

Index